Beautiful Poland

photography:
CHRISTIAN PARMA

text:
MACIEJ KRUPA

The main crest of the High Tatra Mountains, as viewed from the Rusinowa clearing.

landscapes 8

cities 40

churches 72

castles
and palaces 98

folk culture 134

introduction

Any country – including your own homeland – can be viewed from various perspectives. An assessment performed by a geographer or a statistics specialist would seem most common and objective. Such an interpretation typically depicts Poland as one of Europe's largest states, covering an area of approximately 312,000 square kilometres. It is home to over 38 million citizens, of whom 24 million are city-dwellers and just over 14 million live in rural areas. This is a country where for every 100 males there are 106 females; where 10% of its citizens have graduated from university and around 33% have completed secondary education. One might also add that Poland enjoys unrestricted access to the sea, that it borders with seven countries, its territory is divided into 16 provinces and over 2,500 municipalities. In terms of state governance, the lower house of parliament (the Sejm) is supervised by the upper house of parliament (the Senate), and the President acts as head of state; consequently, the Republic of Poland exemplifies a parliamentary democracy. A myriad of figures and data could be quoted at this point, we might sketch maps and enclose charts. Still, it doesn't have to be that way…

For Poland is also a sunrise admired from the seashore; the aroma of the forest after rainfall when the sun, hanging low over the horizon, struggles to pierce down through the branches; it is Wawel Castle gloriously towering over the curve of the Vistula river; and the magnificent snow-capped Tatra Mountains observed from the nearby peaks of Turbacz or Babia Góra. Poland is the languid windings and overflows of the Biebrza river, Kraków's Franciscan basilica's dim interior lit up by stained-glass windows designed by Wyspiański, the mighty oaks and European bison of the Białowieża forest, the narrow alleys of Kazimierz Dolny on the banks of the Vistula river and the white waters of the Dunajec river winding its way through the Pieniny mountains. It is also Kraków's Main Market Square and the Old Town of Warsaw; minuscule wooden Orthodox churches in the Beskid Niski hills and the synagogues of the past surviving in Kraków's Kazimierz district; the poetry of Zbigniew Herbert and Father Baka, music by Henryk Mikołaj Górecki and Bartuś Obrochta, grand canvasses by Jan Matejko and dream-like paintings by Witkacy; Veit Stoss's altar and Our Lady of Krużlowa, the little church in Dębno and the basilica in Licheń.

Multitude in diversity.

For centuries, Polish literature stood on the fringes of the grand literatures: the French, the German, the English and the Russian. In the Polish literary tradition, it is poetry that enjoys greatest significance; prose has never achieved such a level of universality, nor has any Polish novel ever joined the club of European classics. So far, four Poles have been awarded the Nobel Prize for literature – Henryk Sienkiewicz (1905), Władysław Reymont (1924), Czesław Miłosz (1980) and Wisława Szymborska (1996). Stanisław Ignacy Witkiewicz, also known as "Witkacy", the author of novels and plays staged world-wide, was a visionary ahead of his time. Similarly, Witold Gombrowicz was a truly original and universally appreciated writer. But it is poetry that Polish contemporary literature rests upon, with Czesław Miłosz, Wisława Szymborska, Zbigniew Herbert and Tadeusz Różewicz being its brightest stars. Veit Stoss's altar in St. Mary's Church in Kraków remains the most outstanding achievement of the Polish Gothic tradition. However, most great works of the Polish Gothic and Renaissance can best be seen in works of architecture. Most historical architecture in Poland is connected to religion and has been influenced by the Baroque style. Canaletto's paintings praise the glory of 18th-century Warsaw, Marcello Bacciarelli and Piotr Norblin with their inclination for historical and social themes in graphic art laid the foundations for Polish national art. The 19th century witnessed a flourish of Polish painting, marked by the works of Piotr Michałowski, Wojciech Gerson, the Gierymski brothers and, to a great extent, Jan Matejko. At the turn of the 20th century, the prevailing Młoda Polska movement featured Stanisław Wyspiański, Józef Mehoffer, Leon Wyczółkowski and Jacek Malczewski. That is when the Zakopane style of architecture and the applied arts came into being, introduced by its creator – Stanisław Witkiewicz. Among the artists actively operating in the inter-war period, the names of Tadeusz Makowski and Zbigniew Pronaszko deserve particular attention, as well as a Paris-based group of painters representing the Kapist school, and the marvelous "Witkacy", son of Stanisław Witkiewicz, the originator of the Zakopane style. In the second half of the 20th century, Tadeusz Brzozowski and Władysław Hasior seemed of foremost significance for Polish art. Currently it is Magdalena

introduction

Abakanowicz who enjoys the greatest esteem among art connoisseurs worldwide.

Fryderyk Chopin is considered the greatest and most loved Polish composer ever, though the works of Karol Szymanowski are also highly regarded. There also many Polish contemporary composers, whose music is appreciated and performed in concert halls around the world, including Henryk Mikołaj Górecki, the author of the popular *Third Symphony*, Witold Lutosławski and Krzysztof Penderecki. The works of film-music composers Wojciech Kilar and Zbigniew Preisner have featured in many great movies and are considered great compositions in their own right. Poland is also home to many great musicians, such as the pianist Krystian Zimmerman, the jazz trumpeter Tomasz Stańko and the late pianist and composer Krzysztof Komeda.

Polish film-makers have also gained an international reputation for excellence, including the award-winning Roman Polański, who directed *A Knife in the Water*, *Chinatown*, and *Tess*, and *The Pianist*. The late Andrzej Wajda, a prominent representative of the so-called "Polish School" in filmmaking, is the only Polish director to have ever been awarded an honorary Oscar for lifetime achievement. Other great directors include Krzysztof Kieślowski, Marcel Łoziński and Andrzej Fidyk. In the theatre world, Tadeusz Kantor, the founder of Cricot 2 Theatre in Kraków, and Jerzy Grotowski, originator and animator of the Wrocław Laboratorium Theatre, have achieved international recognition. It is also worth mentioning Konrad Swinarski of Teatr Stary (the Old Theatre) in Kraków for his unforgettable staging of *Dziady* by Adam Mickiewicz. Currently, there are also many dynamic alternative theatres, among them Gardzienice, established by Włodzimierz Staniewski, and the Poznań-based Teatr Ósmego Dnia (The Theatre of the Eighth Day).

Should anyone try to draw straight lines to join together the northernmost, southernmost, westernmost and easternmost points of the European continent, these lines would intersect in the heart of Poland. Poland has been located at the crossroads of Europe for many centuries. To the Russians, our country is and used to be perceived as a vestibule of the West, for France and Germany it is a presage of the tempestuous East. For centuries, it was a bulwark of Western Christianity and also a haven of religious tolerance. Polish territory has survived innumerable armed conflicts, including the two World Wars. In the 16th century, the Polish kingdom was a European power, two centuries later as a result of tragic entanglements it was erased from the map of Europe for 123 years. A short period of stability in the inter-war period was followed by the catastrophes of Nazi occupation and Soviet domination. Freedom and democracy resumed in 1989, and not long afterwards Poland regained access to the political and economical structures of a united Europe.

For centuries, Roman and Byzantine influences overlapped in Poland. It is here that basilicas and Orthodox churches were erected, Jewish culture flourished and bore fruit of everlasting value. Cities were established in compliance with German law, and Queen Bona, of Italian descent, laid the foundations for the Polish Renaissance. This is where Copernicus, Marie Skłodowska-Curie and the Nobel Peace Prize laureate Lech Wałęsa were born and active. And finally, this is where Pope John Paul II was born, whose impact upon the image of the contemporary world it is impossible to overestimate.

Poles are relatively immobile; they do not travel extensively and if so they tend to be better acquainted with the monuments of Rome and the seashores of Greece than the enchanting nooks of their native land. Let's take the liberty to pronounce the most banal statement – Poland is an exciting, wonderful and picturesque country. We may not have as many monuments and churches as the Italians, nor as many castles as the French, mountains as the Swiss or beaches as the Greeks do, but owing to the diversity of its landscapes, convoluted paths of history and its location in the heart of Europe, Poland is an attractive country, worthy of in-depth exploration. In this album we aim to present Poland as it is – a country at the crossroads.

The white facade of the Church of the Holy Spirit stands in contrast to its colourful surroundings on Freta street, the main thoroughfare in Warsaw's New Town.

Lake Kórnickie in the Wielkopolska region.

landscapes

Although lowlands notably prevail in Poland, its landscape could on no account be described as homogenous or monotonous. There are beautiful, enchanting corners, sites attractive for their environmental value, as well as breathtaking panoramas all across the country.
The relatively short Baltic seashore itself offers some spectacular vistas. In the west lies the island of Wolin, with its cliffs and national park. At its midpoint lies the Słowiński National Park which astounds visitors with its immense drifting sand-dunes around the town of Łeba. Further to the east the curious wanderer encounters Cape Rozewie, Poland's northernmost tip that is topped with an enormous lighthouse.
And finally, the most emblematic stretch of the Polish seaside: the Hel Peninsula measuring 30 kilometres in length and, at its narrowest point, a mere 200 metres in width. The strip of land separating the Baltic Sea from the Bay of Gdańsk. The Kashubian Switzerland region is famous for its crystal-clear lakes, magnificent forests and and gentle, harmonious landscape. This is where the visitor can find northern Poland's highest hill, Wieżyca (329 m).
The gently undulating regions of Pomerania and the Masurian Lake District abound in post-glacial lakes and enchanting woodlands. Poland's largest (Śniardwy – 109.7 square kilometres) and deepest (Czarna Hańcza – 112 metres deep) lakes can both be found in the Masurian Lake District region.
The Krutynia River is considered to be among the most exquisite water routes, whilst the marshes of the Biebrza river are unrivalled in Europe. This is because the Biebrza river is thought to be the only large European river to have still retained its thoroughly natural character. The Biebrza river overflows without restraint into a wide river basin and meanders freely. There are 150 kilometres of wetlands and innumerable, deep peatbogs that surround the riverbed. For over 10 years, the Biebrza has been Poland's largest national park and also the country's most important bird sanctuary, where over 250 bird species have been observed. Most of them nest in the backwaters of the Biebrza. Elks and beavers also inhabit the nearby woodland areas. The Białowieża Forest is Europe's last remaining primaeval lowland forest. Twenty-five years ago the area was inscribed on the UNESCO World Heritage List. Since 1947, a limited area of the forest, which lies within the Białowieża National Park, has been strictly preserved. This magnificent untouched woodland area is a complex of oaks and hornbeams with a few linden and maple trees. Approximately 2,500 of the trees have been labelled monuments of nature. The forest is home to innumerable preserved species, including a herd of nearly 300 European bison. The species was re-introduced in 1952.
The landscape of Poland's central lowlands is more homogenous; however, the chessboard-like fields, freely winding rivers and roadside willows add charm to this otherwise monotonous panorama. The so-called Błędowska Desert is a rather unusual landscape in this part of the world. However, whilst this sandy area of nearly 30 square kilometres used to be devoid of vegetation, it has recently become increasingly inhabited with plants and has therefore lost some of its distinctive desert look and character. The Krakowsko-Wieluńska Upland, however, is a fascinating region, particularly for its numerous inselbergs. This limestone upland area

landscapes

embraces the Ojcowski National Park and the Prądnik river valley, where one can admire the aptly named "Hercules' Club" rock.
The gentle Świętokrzyskie Mountains are famous for their chief natural attraction: Paradise Cave. It is well lit and open to visitors, who come to admire its wealth of travertine formations. Another tourist spot in the region is the Holy Cross on top of Łysa Góra – formerly the site of a pre-Christian religious cult, currently a Catholic sanctuary and pilgrimage centre.
The Sudety and Carpathian mountain chains stretch across the south of Poland. The highest part of the Sudety range includes the Karkonosze mountains and its highest peak, Śnieżka (1602 m). Besides the Tatras, the Karkonosze are the only alpine mountain range in Poland. They feature innumerable waterfalls and post-glacial cirques, the biggest of which – Śnieżne Kotły – is surrounded by walls towering up to 200 metres high.
The Karkonosze National Park was established so that this area and natural value could be preserved. The Góry Stołowe (Table Mountains), with their phantasmagoric shapes built of sandstone, are another distinctive part of the Sudety chain. The highest peak of the Beskid mountains is Babia Góra (1725 m), Poland's highest mountaintop outside the Tatras.
The Beskids are a chain of relatively low wooded hills, with only a few peaks exceeding the upper forest level. At their easternmost point, close to the border with eastern Slovakia and Ukraine, lie the Bieszczady Mountains. Mountain pastures, known as *Połoniny*, are typical of the region. Many dams have been installed along the highland rivers, forming artificial water reservoirs. The largest of these dams was built on the San river, which created the Soliński Reservoir, a magnificent man-made lake in the foothills of the Bieszczady Mountains.
The Pieniny are a small mountain chain distinguished by particularly picturesque vistas and its main tourist attraction – the Dunajec Gorge. The river fights its way through limestone blocks and this has produced a steep-walled ravine. For 15 kilometres, the river winds its way along seven enormous curves. In one section the river winds for eight kilometres to cover a distance of just three kilometres as the crow flies. The Dunajec river passes the emblematic peaks of the Pieniny – Trzy Korony (Three Crowns) and Sokolica with their characteristic scrub pine trees just below the top. The river is a much-loved location for water-rafting on traditional wooden vessels. The man-made Czorsztyn and Sromowce lakes, completed in 1997, have helped to make the setting of the medieval castles in Czorsztyn and Niedzica even more picturesque. And finally, Poland's mightiest mountain range – the Tatras. Though not particularly extensive, they nevertheless offer a truly alpine panorama. The largest of the lakes in the Polish Tatras – Morskie Oko – is supposedly the most beautiful and is surrounded by steep walls of rock, towering a thousand metres above the surface of the water.
This fabulous amphitheatre of stone, most perfectly visually captures the might and beauty of the Tatras. From the shores of the nearby Czarny Staw (Black Tarn) rises the highest peak of the Polish Tatras – Rysy (2,499 m).
The Gąsienicowa Valley, considered the most enchanting of the valleys in the Tatras, contains 21 tarns, and features breath-taking views towards Orla Perć (the Eagles' Path).
The numerous lakes, streams, waterfalls, caves, karstic springs, post-glacial pot-holes, rock faces and jagged peaks all contribute to the remarkable diversity and heterogeneity of the Tatra landscape – the pride and glory of Polish tourism and one of Poland's best known landscapes.

landscapes

Mixed broadleaved and coniferous forests cover much of the the Łagowski Landscape Park in the Lubuskie Lake District, western Poland.

A bird's-eye view of the Słowiński National Park. This part of the Baltic Coast features large areas of sand dunes that are constantly being shifted and sculpted by the wind.

Wide sandy beaches and dunes on the Baltic coast at Czołpino in the Słowiński National Park.

landscapes

The tall cliffs along the Baltic coast on Wolin island, Western Pomerania, are overgrown with pine forests and offer the most interesting landscapes in the Woliński National Park.

landscapes

The Iława lake district is an extension of the Masurian Lake District and is located between the Vistula and Drwęca rivers. Home to almost 100 lakes set amidst large expanses of forest, it is a popular destination for water sports enthusiasts.

The River Bug meanders its way through the Podlasie Bug Gorge Landscape Park, which features a diverse range of riverbank flora and fauna.

The Biebrza National Park, as seen at sunrise from the bridge in Goniądz.

landscapes

A field of sunflowers in the Łódź region.

The view of Lake Mamry from the well-known sailing centre at Sztynort in the Masurian Lake District.

The arboretum at Kórnik Castle in the Wielkopolska region was established in the nineteenth century and today is home to almost 3,000 varieties and species of trees and shrubs.

landscapes

The Szyja Peninsula extends deep into
Lake Bnińskie in the Wielkopolska region.
A hidden and romantic place today, it was
once a Lusatian culture village and later
a fortified settlement under the Piasts.

landscapes

Quintessentially Polish: willow trees near the village of Młynarze in the Mazovia region.

At the edge of Warsaw. Blossoming poppies along the railway lines in Białołęka.

Paradise Cave, near Kielce, is known for its wealth of cave formations. This picturesque corner gives the impression of a large space – in fact, it is very small.

A picturesque side ravine along the Prądnik valley in the Ojców National Park.

landscapes

This is the traditional agricultural landscape of Poland, visible anywhere from the Baltic Sea to the Tatra Mountains
– a field of maturing cereals swaying gently in the breeze and illuminated by the last rays of the setting sun.

landscapes

This interesting limestone pinnacle in Ogrodzieniec lies in the Eagles' Nests Landscape Park, part of the Kraków-Częstochowa Uplands.

Birch groves such as this one can be found dotted across the diverse landscapes of the Kraków-Częstochowa Uplands.

landscapes

Prądnik Valley, with the 'Kraków Gate' limestone formation on the far side, as viewed from Ciemna cave.

The majestic Trzy Korony [Three Crowns] massif towers above the Dunajec river gorge in the Pieniny mountains.

The Podhale region. Late summer on Gubałówka hill.

landscapes

Beneath the peaks of the Tatras. In Biały Potok clearing,
the pale purple crocuses herald the arrival of spring.

The High Tatras. Bad weather in the mountains may be a thing of beauty – here Mnich and Zadni Mnich tower above Morskie Oko lake.

The Western Tatras. The view from Sucha Przełęcz towards Beskid – where the state border is marked out by posts.

landscapes

The foothills of the Tatras.
The mountains as they appear
from Głodówka clearing, beside
the road to Morskie Oko lake.

Toruń. The Monument to Copernicus in the Old Town Market Square.

cities

Historians of religion claim that every new human settlement is, in a sense, a re-creation of the world. Building a new city recurrently repeats the scheme of bringing the world into being. This is the underlying foundation of cities, which have a clearly specified structure and order. This scheme relates, in particular, to older cities which have, to some extent, retained their original layout. Typically, in Europe the city centre used to be occupied by a church or a market square; and surrounded by walls that were both defensive and symbolic in meaning – they isolated the city from the adjoining space and chaos. Urban centres of today tend to repeat that pattern, although they may occasionally form several central points encircled with new residential and industrial boroughs. Kraków's Old Town is perhaps the best example of this medieval urban layout. Kraków was built in compliance with the Magdeburg city law. It was encircled with a green area (Planty), and built around the central point of the Main Market Square (the largest square in Medieval Europe), on which stood the Town Hall and the Cloth Hall. Wawel Castle overlooks the whole city. Remnants of the city's fortification walls have survived to today, including Florian Gate and the Barbican.

Another circumferential layer of buildings around Planty clearly shows the stages of development that the city experienced, expanding around its medieval centre. Kazimierz, a district of Kraków that used to be a fully independent settlement, was one of the main centres of the Jewish Diaspora in Europe, and as such features a wealth of historic monuments, synagogues and churches, charming narrow alleys and little squares. On the other hand, Nowa Huta, another of Kraków's districts, is the only Polish settlement that was built according to the principles of socialist realist architecture and much of its original urban layout remains. Toruń's Old and New Town are an example of a perfectly preserved historical urban layout. Due to the city's numerous buildings and structures of great historical value, Toruń was inscribed on the UNESCO World Heritage List. The layout and arrangement of Toruń's Main Market Square, with its town hall, monument of Copernicus and the home of the great scientist, as well as the Gothic buildings and fortifications along the Vistula river's waterfront are considered priceless. The Royal Way in Gdańsk is the city's central artery. It is composed of two avenues: Długi Targ (Long Market) and Ulica Długa (Long Street). It is here that the Town Hall, the Neptune Fountain and the Artus Court are situated – a testimony to the wealth and might of Gdańsk's townsmen. The Żuraw [Crane] is a reminder of Gdańsk's long tradition as a harbour, and that it used to play the dual role of port facility and city gates. The medieval urban layout of Sandomierz, a cliff settlement overlooking the Vistula river, has also survived until today. This includes the main market square, the town hall, the fortifications, the complex network of underground tunnels, the Romanesque church of Saint Jacob, and a historical house that was inhabited by the royal chronicler Jan Długosz. The sightseeing monuments of Łódź are chiefly associated with the city's industrial heritage and most of them are located on or close to Piotrkowska Street

cities

— Europe's longest commercial avenue. The street features many buildings in the Classicist and Secessionist styles, including the opulent palaces built by the wealthy factory owners: Scheibler and Poznański. For years, the atmosphere and architecture of Łódz was shaped by the interweaving of the Polish, German and Jewish cultures that were present here. Poland's capital, Warsaw, is a city that underwent comprehensive reconstruction after being utterly demolished during the Second World War. The recreated old part of the metropolis comprises the Castle Square with the Royal Castle, Sigismund's Column, the Old and the New Town, countless parks and palaces. The new downtown part, encircling the socialist realist Palace of Science and Culture and dominated by contemporary skyscrapers, acts as a counterpoint to Warsaw's Old Town. Wrocław's Old Town was also restored after the Second World War. The medieval town hall, which stands at the very centre of the Main Market Square, is one of the most sumptuous secular buildings of medieval Europe. Zamość is exceptional among Poland's cities. It was established in 1580 by hetman Jan Zamoyski, who ordered that an 'ideal city' be built according to the principles of Renaissance architecture. The city has three entrance gates and within the city's walls visitors can admire the Main Market Square with the centrally raised Town Hall, two minor squares, a collegiate church, an Orthodox church transformed into a Catholic temple and a synagogue, Zamoyski's palace and the Zamość Academy. The city layout was designed by the Italian Bernardo Morando.

Poland is also home to many enchanting little towns, sharing harmonious, often historical architecture. One such example is Kazimierz Dolny, which lies beside the Vistula river. Its market square contains one of the most magnificent Renaissance houses in Poland, with a richly ornamented facade and a splendid attic. The rest of the architecture in this small town is mostly traditional and includes the churches of Saint John the Baptist and Saint Bartholomew, as well as some delightful 16th and 17th century granaries. Another small town with a medieval layout is Stary Sącz with its Saint Clare's convent and church, founded in the 13th century by Saint Kinga. The market square is encircled by peculiar, manor-style houses. In Poland innumerable historical settlements declined and lost their significance; many became villages. On the other hand, post-war urban development led to the creation of new towns and cities where pre-fabricated blocks of flats, chaos, ugliness and an overall lack of distinct individuality prevailed. In more recent years, however, standards of architecture, building materials and technology have improved immeasurably and many new buildings, such as concert halls, museums, stadiums, residential and office buildings have been recognised and awarded international prizes. Nonetheless, places such as Kraków, Toruń, Stary Sącz and Tykocin have managed to preserve the spirit of their townsfolk, architects and engineers of the past. This is where you can feel the harmonious, familiar and human heartbeat of every city representing the world in miniature.

Szczecin's new iconic philharmonic concert hall, built in 2014. Despite the building's innovative shape, it has been cleverly integrated into its historical surroundings.

Long Market, Gdańsk. The Neptune fountain dating from 1633 stands in front of the brick Gothic town hall, baroque town houses and the Renaissance facade of the Artus Court.

The medieval port crane beside the Motlawa River in Gdańsk.

This fairytale-like Crooked House was built in the popular seaside resort of Sopot in 2004, and has since become very popular with holidaymakers.

cities

Poznań's Old Town Market Square. The Renaissance-style Town Hall is topped off by a tall attic depicting the town's walls, plus a slender tower. In the foreground – the Apollo fountain, one of four fountains located on the market square.

Toruń. The Artus Court was built at the end of the 19th century as a meeting place for merchants and a centre of social life. Today it is a branch of the Gdańsk History Museum. The floodlighting reveals many of the artistic features on the building's Neo-Renaissance facade.

Warsaw. The view of the city from the right side of the Vistula river. Modern tower blocks loom over the older buildings. Despite the arrival of a lot of new buildings in recent years, the capital's tallest building remains the Socialist Realist-style Palace of Culture and Science from 1955.

Warsaw's modern centre – a view from the window of the 190-metre-high "Złota 44" apartment building; (from left to right) the skyscrapers "Rondo I", "Q" and "Spektrum" and part of the Warsaw Financial Centre building.

Castle Square, Warsaw. Painstakingly rebuilt after the Second World War, the Old Town, Royal Castle and Sigismund III Waza Column.

Łódź, Piotrkowska Street. The open-air Gallery of Great Inhabitants of Łódź is a series of sculptures cast in bronze and laid out along the street. The men near the table are the *Founders of Industrial Łódź*, i.e. Izrael Poznański, Karol Scheibler and Ludwik Grohmann.

Kazimierz Dolny. The view from Krzyżowa hill over the town picturesquely located beside the Vistula river. This old small town began to be frequented by artists in the 19th century.

Zamość, an ideal Renaissance city. Armenian street, which leads to the side wall of the Town Hall and the northern side of the Great Market Square.

cities

Lublin. An interesting view over the roofs of the Old Town, the Gothic-style Kraków Gate with its Baroque helmet-roof, and the neo-Classical town hall with its colonnaded portico, as viewed from Trynitarska Tower.

Wrocław. Tumski Bridge and Cathedral Street lead onto Ostrów Tumski island, and to the monumental Gothic-style Cathedral of John the Baptist, whose two multi-storey towers dominate the surroundings.

Wrocław, the University and former Jesuit College. The *Aula Leopoldina* is a Baroque masterpiece from the years 1728-1741; sculpture, plasterwork, wall paintings and wood carvings together create an iconographic image that glorifies wisdom, knowledge and science.

cities

Katowice, Nikiszowiec. The narrow streets and dense building of the redbrick tenement houses confer a unique atmosphere upon this workers' estate.

Kraków, Nowa Huta district. The beauty of industrial space in the now defunct *Zgniatacz* rolling mill of the old Lenin Steelworks (subsequently the Sendzimira works and now the Kraków branch of ArcelorMittal Poland S.A.).

Kraków. The asymmetrical Gothic-style towers of Saint Mary's Church loom over the Main Market Square. At the square's centre is the Cloth Hall – originally a Gothic-style building, which now also features Renaissance ornamentation and neo-Gothic style arcades.

Kraków. The view from the tower of Saint Mary's Church over the roofs of the Old Town towards Wawel hill with its cathedral and castle.

Szeroka street in Kraków's Kazimierz district. The wooden shop signs are an attempt to restore the pre-War character of what was formerly a not very well-off Jewish quarter.

Zakopane. Krupówki street is probably Poland's most famous pedestrian thoroughfare. This resort town at the foot of the Tatra Mountains is prized for the tourist and recreational opportunities it offers.

Warsaw. The statue of *Christ Carrying the Cross* stands in front of the Holy Cross Church.

churches

The cultural purpose of temples has always been associated with symbolising the centre of the world – understood as the micro-world of the village or town. Temples sanctified space, served as a landmark and organised all things in an architectural, symbolic and spiritual sense. They served as the axis mundi – the axis of the world, where heaven meets earth. This cultural role of churches gave birth to their dominance both in the Polish landscape and in Poland's cultural heritage.

When attempting to describe Poland's numerous churches we have to start with the most important temple in the Polish-Lithuanian Commonwealth – Wawel Cathedral. There is a powerful bond between the history of this cathedral and the past of both the castle and Poland. The current cathedral was built in the 14th century on the remains of two former Romanesque churches that originally stood on Wawel Hill. It gradually became encircled with multitudinous chapels, including the masterpiece of the Polish Renaissance – the Sigismund Chapel, which is the burial place of Polish sovereigns, political leaders and the greatest national poets.

Another of Kraków's prominent places of worship – Saint Mary's Church on the Main Market Square – was built at the turn of the 14th century. It is commonly regarded to be the very heart of old Kraków. The church is adorned with the renowned Gothic altar by Veit Stoss and from its tower an hourly bugle-call has been played daily for over 600 years.

The panorama of Kraków's Old Town is a magnificent skyline of church towers with multitudinous architectural styles. From Romanesque elements in the churches of Saint Isidore and Saint Wojciech, through the classical Gothic basilicas of Franciscan and Dominican Friars, to the Baroque buildings of Saint Anne's and Saints Peter and Paul.

The Monastery of Jasna Góra is particularly cherished by Polish Catholics. The basilica with the Chapel of the Mother of God of Częstochowa and the Paulites' Monastery are among the most frequently visited sites in Poland, and the destination of innumerable pilgrimages. It is here that the Sacred Likeness of the Black Madonna is exhibited. Jasna Góra was the sole speck of Poland that did not surrender to the Swedish Deluge of the 17th century, which helped to reinforce its exceptional meaning and establish itself as the spiritual capital of Poland.

The Archcathedral of Gniezno on Lech's Hill is the cradle of the Polish Catholic Church. It is here that Saint Adalbert, the martyr and patron of Poland, was buried and the first Polish sovereign – Bolesław the Brave – was crowned. The Romanesque gateway to the temple is a priceless monument of early Polish medieval art. In Poznań, on the island of Ostrów Tumski, stands the Archcathedral Basilica, the seat of the first Polish bishopric and the mausoleum of the first Polish rulers – Mieszko I and Bolesław

churches

the Brave. The 12th-century Romanesque church of Saint Procopius and the Romanesque pillars in the Baroque temple of the Holy Trinity, that have survived in Strzelno near Gniezno, are among the oldest religious buildings in Poland.
Saint Mary's Church in Gdańsk is the pride and joy of the city and proof of the immense wealth of the city's burghers. The Gothic altar of Saint Anne's Chapel with the statue of the Beautiful Madonna and a copy of Hans Memling's *Last Judgement* all deserve close attention. There are other grand religious buildings in Pomerania, including the Gothic Co-Cathedral Basilica in Kołobrzeg, and cathedrals in Kwidzyn, Frombork and Pelplin. There are also many modern churches, such as the Lord's Ark and the Mistrzejowice church in the Nowa Huta district of Kraków. Regrettably, most contemporary religious buildings in Poland are not particularly good-looking and therefore cannot be considered among the masterpieces of Polish architecture, though in recent years the standards have, in general, improved and buildings in Poland are now starting to be recognized and win international prizes. Poland's largest contemporary church is the basilica in Licheń.

In contrast to the grand churches of brick or stone, the Polish countryside is home to many charming wooden church buildings. In the foothills of the Tatra Mountains, one can find several fine Gothic wooden churches. One of them is Saint Michael the Archangel's church in Dębno near Nowy Targ, which is particularly valuable for its gorgeous 15th-century wall-painting and unique, regional-style internal design. The churches of Orawka, in the Orawa region, and Trybsz, in the Spis region, both feature exceptionally fine wall-paintings and rich ornamentation. In Zakopane, apart from the simple Old Church on Kościeliska street, one can also encounter the chapel in Jaszczurówka designed by Stanisław Witkiewicz in accordance with the principles of the Zakopane Style. An old wooden church in Rabka has been transformed into a regional museum. In Karpacz, on the other hand, one can find the 13th-century wooden Wang church that was transported to Karpacz from its original location in Norway. The numerous non-Catholic places of worship in Poland are evidence of the constant presence of religious minorities in the country. They are part of the heritage of religious diversity shared by the Republic of the Two Nations and the Second Republic of Poland. For centuries, Poland was a melting pot of various ethnic and religious groups, a land of tolerance and diverse cultural and religious traditions based on equal rights. In Kruszyniany and Bohoniki, near Białystok, one may still find old Tatar mosques. The eastern and southern regions of Poland are inhabited by members of the Eastern Orthodox congregation and Greek Catholics. Numerous Orthodox churches of the region include the most renowned of this kind in Poland erected on Grabarka mountain. In the Mazuria region one can also encounter a "molenna", or a prayer house of the Old Believers. Synagogues can still be found in the country's large cities and provincial towns. Seven synagogues have survived in Kraków's Kazimierz district, including the Old Synagogue that contains a museum of Jewish culture. Protestant churches can also be found In the regions of Silesia, Wielkopolska, Warmia and Mazuria.

A church, synagogue or Tatar mosque has always been at the heart of local existence – in the centre of the city, town or village. It is around them that all activity took place. It still does, although many religious sites today are a mere reminder of their past glory and cultural meaning.

Gniezno. The view down Tumska Street is closed off by the Gothic Cathedral of the Assumption of Mary, with its two massive towers and its chancel ringed by chapels. The famous Gniezno Doors are mounted in the southern portal.

Pelplin. The Cathedral of the Blessed Virgin Mary retains its original Gothic-style stalls, and the Baroque High Altar is also interesting, featuring the *Coronation of Mary* by Hermann Hahn.

Gdańsk-Oliwa. The Gothic cathedral is famous for its organ, which was constructed in Johann Wilhelm Wulff's workshop between the years 1763-1788. It includes many moving elements. The plasterwork clouds with cherubic heads above the altar conceal some of the organ pipes.

Gniezno. The silver confessional holds relics of Saint Adalbert. It dates back to the 17th century and is the work of the Gdańsk-based goldsmith Peter von der Rennen. It was placed in the chancel, under a canopy supported by gilded Solomon-style columns.

Licheń Stary. This small locality near Konin achieved fame through its sanctuary centring around the cult of the miraculous painting of the Licheń Mother of God. The giant new basilica here is in fact Poland's largest church.

Płock. The marble sarcophagus of the King of Poland Władysław Herman is in the Renaissance Cathedral's Royal Chapel. The Cathedral stands for all to see on the Tumski Mound above the Vistula river.

Henryków. The makeover of the formerly Cistercian church here gave it a homogeneous Baroque-style decor. Around 1710, the church gained Silesia's most magnificent stalls, based on Dutch originals, with exquisite wood-carving and stylised sculpturework.

churches

Wrocław. The porch to the Gothic-style Cathedral of Saint John the Baptist on Ostrów Tumski island features mounted Romanesque columns from the site's former place of worship.

Świdnica. The Evangelical Church of Peace dates from the mid-seventeenth century. Its interior is surrounded by two floors of wooden loges and galleries.

Lubiąż. The great Baroque monastery complex appeared between 1681 and 1720, comprising a Gothic-style church partly made over in the Baroque, as well as two wings in the form of the monastery and the Abbot's Palace. The Palace's Prince's Room is adorned by Franz Joseph Mangoldt's sculptures.

Częstochowa. The Church of the Assumption of the Blessed Virgin Mary within the sanctuary of Jasna Góra. Shown here is the procession to the Chapel of Saint Paul the First Hermit, patron of the Pauline Order.

churches

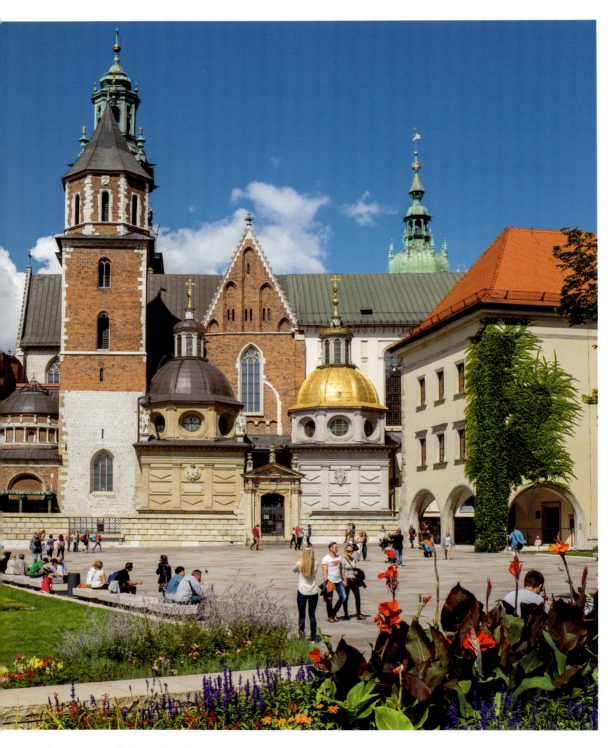

Kraków's Wawel Hill. The Cathedral of Saints Stanisław and Wacław is ringed by chapels. The Renaissance Sigismund Chapel on the south side is the work of Bartolomeo Berrecci, while the Baroque-style Waza Chapel is also modelled on it.

Kraków. The main altar of the Gothic-style Saint Mary's Church dates back to the years 1477-1489 and was built by Veit Stoss of Nuremberg. The Neo-Gothic polychromy was added in the 19th century by the acclaimed painters Jan Matejko, Józef Mehoffer and Stanisław Wyspiański.

churches

Kraków, Nowa Huta. The Mother of God, Queen of Poland Church is known as the Lord's Ark. Designed by Wojciech Pietrzyk, it was built in the years 1967-1977. The expressive eight-metre-tall crucifix was sculpted by Bronisław Chromy.

Kwiatoń, the Łemko Orthodox church of Saint Paraskevi built in the 17th century is among the most beautiful of the wooden churches in the Subcarpathia region.

Binarowa, the Church of Saint Michael the Archangel from around 1500. The walls of the chancel are decorated with scenes of the Passion of Christ, and in the Baroque altar there is a Gothic-style Mother of God with Child.

Rabka. The old Church of Saint Mary Magdalene was built of wooden logs in 1606. It today houses the Władysław Orkan Regional Museum.

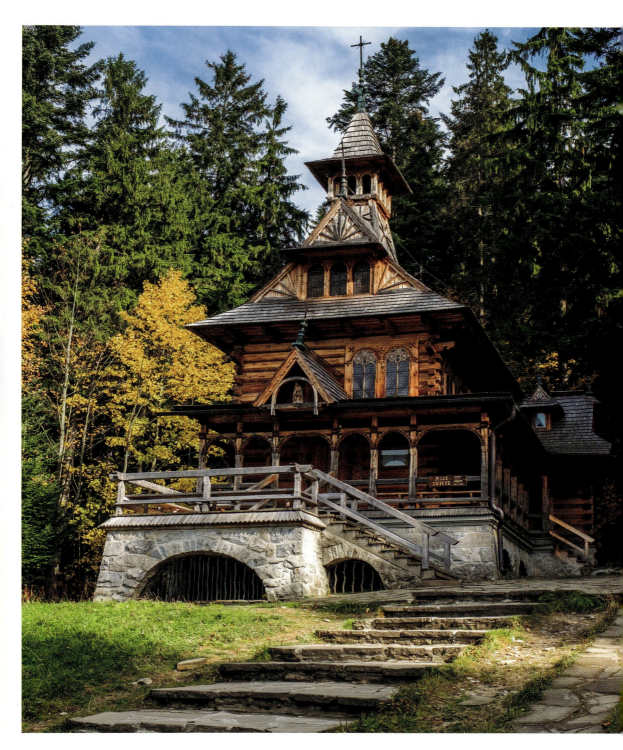

Zakopane. The wooden chapel at Jaszczurówka was designed by
Stanisław Witkiewicz in the Zakopane Style and built from 1904 to 1908.

Walewice. The Neo-Classical palace here was designed by Hilary Szpilowski and built in the late 18th century. It is perhaps best known as the site of the romance between Maria Walewska and Napoleon Bonaparte.

castles and palaces

Castles and palaces frequently appear in the Polish landscape. Initially they were wooden constructions; these have, however, not survived to our time. The first stone fortifications and residential buildings emerged in the 13th century in the Małopolska region, but the majority of medieval castles were built in the 14th century. This is when the fortified strongholds of Niedzica and Czorsztyn (now a ruin) were constructed along the Dunajec River. Many fortifications can be found along the border of the regions of Małopolska and Silesia, on the limestone Krakowsko-Wieluńska Uplands. In the era of King Casimir the Great, enormous stone strongholds were erected in the area, among others in the vicinity of Olsztyn, Ogrodzieniec, Mirów, Chęciny and Bobolice. These constructions typically featured fortified walls and towers. Regrettably, most of them today lie in ruins. With the exception of Wawel castle, the only preserved and intact fortified castle in the region is Pieskowa Skała, which was reconstructed during the Renaissance era. The Silesian castles, e.g. in Bolkowo or Będzin, constitute a separate group of medieval strongholds. The magnificent fortress in Brzeg served for many years as the seat of the Silesian branch of the Piast dynasty. However, the largest stronghold in Silesia, and the third in size among all Polish castles, is the Książ (Fürstenstein) Castle. Originally built in the 13th century, it was later remade in the Renaissance and Baroque styles and was transformed from a fort into the residence of a noble family. Other significant fortresses of Silesia include the strongholds in Głogów, Oleśnica, Otmuchów, the eclectic castle of Moszna and the castle of Czocha, near Leśna. On the Polish lowlands, bricks from Pomerania and Prussia were the main building material. The main stronghold of the region is at Malbork (Marienburg) where Europe's largest Gothic fortress was built by the Teutonic Knights. Other significant defensive structures built by the Teutonic Order include Kwidzyn (Marienwerder), Lidzbark Warmiński (Heilsberg), Frombork (Frauenburg) and Braniewo (Braunsberg). The Kwidzyn (Marienwerder) castle and cathedral is deemed to be one of the most magnificent fortified constructions of the late Middle Ages. The Teutonic, later Polish, castle in Golub-Dobrzyń (Gollub) has been preserved in excellent condition. Though dilapidated, the ruins of Krzyżtopór castle in the Kielce region are impressive nonetheless. Erected in the early 17th century, this castle is one of the largest in Europe, and used to be owned by the noble Ossoliński family. In the spirit of the time, the building reflected the ordering of time and of the universe. It had 365 windows, 52 chambers, 12 halls and 4 towers. Krzyżtopór survived for a mere 11 years before it was destroyed during the Swedish Deluge. The castle in Krąg near Koszalin shared the same "cosmic" pattern. Royal residences deserve a separate portrayal. Wawel Castle was for over 500 years the home of Polish sovereigns. Its main Gothic edifice was erected by Casimir the Great, extended by Władysław Jagiełło and given a Renaissance-style facelift during the reign of Sigismund the Elder. Its wonderful location in the centre of Kraków, its splendid collection of Arras tapestries, and its many styles from many epochs, make Wawel one of the most beautiful and frequently visited castles in Poland. Warsaw's Royal Castle, on the other hand, was not only the residence of sovereigns as from the beginning of the 16th century, but it was also a meeting place for parliamentary debates. Demolished during the Second World War, the castle was rebuilt in the 1970s. Apart from redecorating Warsaw's Royal Castle, Poland's rulers also liked to build their private suburban residences. Jan III Sobieski built a magnificent manor house in Wilanów, considered

castles and palaces

a jewel of Polish Baroque architecture with a tremendous art gallery, wonderful ornaments, fittings and gardens. The last Polish king, Stanisław Augustus Poniatowski, left us with his summer Palace on the Island in the Royal Łazienki Park. Nieborów, near Łowicz is the site of a magnificent complex of palaces and parks, erected by the Radziwiłł family, famous for its vast art collection and landscaped garden – Arcadia. Łańcut castle, on the other hand, owes its current shape to the Lubomirski family, who remade the building in the 18th century in the Classicist and Rococo styles, with a concert hall and a theatre. Today, the complex serves as a museum exhibiting, among others, the largest collection of carriages in Poland. Another prominent aristocratic residence is the hunting mansion in Pszczyna, in the region of Silesia, which was remade many times over the years. Its last makeover took place in the 19th century when it adopted many of the French architectural designs of the time. The mansion in Pszczyna can be compared with the most renowned European palaces. The castle in Baranów near Sandomierz is sometimes referred to as "little Wawel" as it exemplifies the architectural ideas of the late Renaissance in its full bloom.

The Wielkopolska region also offers several fascinating buildings, including the early 19th-century wooden hunting mansion in Antonin, the 16th-century castle in Gołuchów, that was later reconstructed in the Renaissance style and set in English-style landscaped parklands. The palace and park of Kórnik were the property of Władysław Zamoyski. Rogalin is famous for its mansion, representing a mixture of Rococo and Classicist styles, and its ancient oaks growing in the park. Castles and palaces are tightly bound up with the tradition of Polish collections. Poland's oldest art collections are the royal collections, including the magnificent set of Arras tapestries collected by King Sigismund Augustus, exhibited at Wawel castle and in the Warsaw branch of the National Museum. Rulers of the Vasa dynasty were equally keen collectors, especially Sigismund III, Władysław IV and John Casimir. Similarly, chancellor Jerzy Ossoliński and King Jan III Sobieski shared a passion for collecting. Many Polish art collections were decimated during the era of partitions. Establishing public museums was near impossible at that time, though one of the few exceptions to this rule was the Museum of Fine Arts, which was founded in Warsaw in 1862 and later transformed into the National Museum. Kraków has always been considered an important place for collecting, with its precious collections at the Polish Academy of Skills and the Jagiellonian University. The liberal policy of the Austrian partition authorities made it possible to found the Kraków branch of the National Museum in 1879. Poznań, Toruń and Lwów hosted prominent art collections as well. Grand private art collections were also gathered by families such as the Działyńskis in Kórnik, the Raczyńskis in Rogalin, the Czartoryskis in Gołuchów, the Zamoyskis in Zamość and the Krasińskis in Warsaw. The late 19th century witnessed the emergence of regional museums. The Tatra Museum in Zakopane, which was founded in 1889, was the first establishment of this kind. The Contemporary Art Museum in Łódz has managed to compile one of the finest collections of modern art in Poland. Poland's numerous castles, palaces and ruins are a testimony to the country's past glory and might. They are monuments of its cultural diversity, openness to the world, wealth and the influence of their former proprietors. Some of the buildings were returned to their lawful heirs, the majority were transformed into museums exhibiting valuable collections of historical arts and crafts. They are an indispensable element of both the urban and rural Polish landscape.

Łódź, the Mansion of Edward Herbst dating back to 1875. The oriental decor of the Yellow Room in this mansion of the Łódź industrialist was filled with furniture, ceramics and textiles from the Far East.

Malbork (Marienburg). This fortress on the River Nogat has a multifaceted collection of Gothic-style buildings first erected between the last quarter of the 13th century and the second half of the 15th. It was the seat of power and formal capital of the state run by the Order of the Teutonic Knights.

Malbork (Marienburg). The Gothic trifolium of the cloisters is crowned by fine tracery supported on small decorative columns. This is an example of the many works of mediaeval art at this largest brick-built castle in Europe.

castles and palaces

Radzyń Chełmiński (Reden). The picturesque ruin of the mid-14th century Gothic castle of the Teutonic Knights, which was restored in the early 20th century.

Kórnik. The castle here was remodelled in the mid-19th century, the result being a beautiful Neo-Gothic structure based on the design by Karl Friedrich Schinkel. The interiors were also much upgraded – the impressive doorway offers a view into the dining room.

Koło. The ruins of the 14th-century Royal Castle, built above the banks of the River Warta in the Gothic style, which once guarded the then northern border with Brandenburg and the state of the Teutonic Knights.

Warsaw. The Throne Room is one of the most sumptuous and beautiful chambers of Warsaw's Royal Castle. The throne is adorned with silver eagles embroidered with silver thread.

castles and palaces

Warsaw's Wilanów Palace was the summer residence of King Jan III Sobieski, and takes the form of an 18th-century palace/garden complex. The most imposing principal facade is decorated with *bas-reliefs* and allegorical statuary designed to pay homage to the military successes of the hero-King.

Nieborów. The Baroque-style palace, designed by Tilman van Gameren, is one of the most precious historical buildings in the Masovia region. The preserved interiors, such as the "Green Room" which once served as a boudoir, are from the 18th and 19th centuries.

castles and palaces

Łódź. The palace built for the industrialist Izrael Poznański in the late 19th and early 20th centuries was used for residential, promotional and commercial purposes. Its Neo-Baroque style Dining Room with plasterwork décor is especially beautiful.

Wojanów. Set in parkland and now serving as an elegant hotel, Wojanów Hall is a fantastic Renaissance/Neo-Gothic-style construction flanked by round towers.

castles and palaces

Rabsztyn is one of the castles along the so-called Jura Fortresses trail. The ruin is impressive enough to remind us how huge the original castle was – in its heyday it comprised a Mediaeval upper castle plus a 17th-century lower one, taking the form of a three-winged palace.

Mirów. The remains of the Gothic castle here today provides a picturesque addition to the Jurassic limestone landscape.

Zagórze Śląskie. Located on raised land, the Gothic-Renaissance Grodno Castle was built of stone and brick between the 13th and 16 th centuries. One of the castle's attractions today is a woman's skeleton chained to the wall after being condemned to death for treachery and manslaughter.

castles and palaces

Książ (Fürstenstein). The two-storey Baroque-style Maksymilian Hall is in the more showy eastern wing of the castle, and was formerly used as a ballroom.

Brzeg. The 13th-century castle of the Silesian Piasts was made subject to a thorough remodelling in the Renaissance period. Its internal arcaded courtyard has been likened to the castle in Kraków, and is sometimes called 'the Silesian Wawel'.

Pszczyna. The Palace of the Hochberg Princes of Pless. The two-floor Mirror Room – the largest in the Pszczyna Palace – served as a dining room. The interiors were further illuminated by huge mirrors and crystal chandeliers.

castles and palaces

Kliczków. The present palace stands on the site of a former stronghold used to defend the border in the 13th century. It was transformed into a Renaissance-style manor house three centuries later, only for the residence to be rebuilt and given a multi-towered Neo-Renaissance appearance at the end of the 19th century.

Moszna. The great eclectic palace from the late 19th and early 20th centuries has 99 larger or smaller towers, and wings in the Neo-Gothic, Neo-Renaissance and Neo-Baroque styles. The architect designed it with 365 rooms.

Kraków. The view of Wawel hill from the Vistula river. The complex of buildings is dominated by Sigismund's Clock and "Silver Bells" towers belonging to the Cathedral. The Royal Castle is out of sight beyond the Austrian barracks.

castles and palaces

Czorsztyn. This picturesquely located Gothic-style ruined castle once monitored traffic and trade along the Dunajec river.

Niedzica. This fortress was built of broken stone and comprises Gothic-style upper and lower castles, as well as a Renaissance-style middle one. Legend has it that the answer to a puzzle about hidden Inca gold is hidden somewhere in this castle.

Łańcut. The oft-remodelled castle here lost its defensive function long ago. Today it is a beautiful palace surrounded by gardens and a landscaped park. The Neo-Baroque-style former coach-house holds a unique collection of carriages and sleighs.

castles
and palaces

Krasiczyn. The 16th-century Renaissance castle of the Krasicki family took 50 years to remodel into the Mannerist style. The corners of the square-shaped residence are flanked by the cylindrical Royal, Noble, Divine and Papal towers.

Kozłówka. Marble staircase from the turn of the 19th and 20th centuries featuring Neo-Rococo forged balustrades and intricate stucco work.

Łowicz. During the feast of Corpus Christi, the town's streets are filled with colourful processions.

folk culture

Poland's flourishing folk culture distinguishes itself from the majority of Western states. Folklore is the compilation of everyday and festive traditions and customs; a collection of beliefs and religious practices; folk art and craft; music, dance and literature. Folk culture is structured according to the rites connected with celebrations organised in accordance with two cycles – the annual passage of seasons and family events.

In the Advent period, initiating the liturgical year, remnants of old ceremonies are present in games and fortune-telling on Saint Andrew's Day (November 30th) and in the custom of exchanging gifts on Saint Nicholas' Day (December 6th). However, the most emblematic holiday of all is the celebration of Christmas, joining popular elements of Christmas Eve such as the family supper, decorating the Christmas tree, participating in midnight mass, exchanging presents and singing carols. It is typical of some regions that Christmas nativity scenes are arranged or carol singers perform in public. It is typical of some regions that Christmas nativity scenes are arranged or carol singers perform in public. The subsequent carnival period has lost much of its meaning as a transition time between the joyous Christmas and subdued Lent.

The spring festivities of Easter are rich in symbolic rites. In certain regions, Palm Sunday is celebrated with the making of imposingly tall Easter Palms, some of them exceeding several metres in height. In churches the symbolic Tomb of Christ is usually arranged and often provided with a guard. The three days of Easter celebrations is a time when Mystery Plays recreating Christ's Via Dolorosa are performed, the most renowned of these is the one held in Kalwaria Zebrzydowska. Easter would not be the same without the blessing of food ceremony on Holy Saturday, the Resurrection mass, decorated Easter Eggs or the *Śmigus-dyngus* ritual.

May is a time of evening devotions to the Blessed Mary often held around roadside shrines. The Polish celebrations of Corpus Christi, eight weeks after Easter, are truly festive in character and feature colourful processions. The night of Saint John's, heralding the approaching summer, abounds in pre-Christian symbols associated with the cult of fire and the passage of time. All Saints' Day (November 1st) is when Poles traditionally visit the last resting-place of their ancestors, they decorate graves and light symbolic candles. These customs have a unique character in Poland and are unlike anywhere else in Europe.

Family holidays – baptism celebrations, First Communion, weddings – are also marked with specific rites and customs. Weddings in particular, their ritual and specified order, include a multitude of ancient customs and symbols; for this reason weddings are usually the best representation of local culture, rich in word, music and dance.

The most conspicuous element of material folk culture is the style of architecture. Numerous residential and farm buildings are a testimony to past architectural traditions of the region. Folk churches and chapels, often of supreme value, should not be forgotten here, as well as roadside shrines and crosses. Initially, folk art was of a purely pragmatic character; sculptures, paper cutouts and paintings were used as decorations in countryside churches and

cottages. Gradually, it advanced to become a fully autonomous phenomenon of Polish folklore and folk sculptures, and Highlanders' glass-painting found their way to art exhibitions and museums. Until today, church fairs have retained their festive quality and unify the village community. Festivals of folk culture are an opportunity for local song and dance ensembles to present their regional customs, dances and songs and are a novelty. The mass participation in pilgrimages, especially those in August to the Monastery of Jasna Góra, exemplifies the folk spiritual tradition.

Due to historical transformations such as the processes of urban development and mass migration, folk culture is vanishing and its character has been altered. Folk traditions remain alive and well, however, in the regions of Podhale, Kurpie, Silesia, around Łowicz and Rzeszów. In many regions, local customs are being revived and the folk traditions of the past are restored, often for theatrical purposes. In the Podhale region, one can still encounter Highlander costumes and dances, listen to Highlander music and song. Regional folk ensembles are active; they play local music and teach the eager youth the old traditions of their predecessors. Glass-painting, sculpting, wood-carving and violin-making are perhaps most alive and popular in the Podhale region. Many such artists are also appreciated abroad. The wedding procession led by *pytace* – horsemen invited to the wedding reception – is still common in Podhale. Sundays and festive occasions are frequently marked with people wearing regional Highlander costume. Local restaurants offer Highlander dishes and joyful Highland music to accompany the food. The area's shepherding remains alive and well – mountain pastures and glades are used for traditional sheep-grazing and the sound of shepherds' bells echoes amid the mountain clearings and forests. Original folk culture at its best is a major attraction luring visitors to Zakopane and the Podhale region. Poland remains one of the last countries in Europe to retain its living folk culture. Folklore remains the pride and joy of many communities and is passed on from generation to generation. Castles and palaces are a reminder of the country's aristocracy, the cities are a testimony to the burghers' traditions, while folklore perpetuates the customs of small-town peasantry – an indispensable part of Poland's national culture.

Dziekanowice, by Lake Lednica. Wielkopolska-style windmills, saved from neglect, have been given a new lease of life at the ethnographic park here.

Zalipie. The "Painted Village", where local tradition dictates that houses, other buildings and household items should all be painted.

Górka Klasztorna. This small locality in the Wielkopolska region is the oldest Sanctuary of Our Lady in Poland. Each year at Easter it hosts a mystery play which culminates in the Crucifixion scene.

folk culture

On the first Saturday of August events are held to commemorate the settlement here of incomers from Bamberg in Franconia. On this day, women wear traditional costumes with beautiful flower-laden caps.

The District Museum of the Kalisz region in Russów is an outdoor museum that brings together traditional architecture and household items to illustrate the conditions experienced by moderately well-off peasant families of the late 19th and early 20th centuries.

folk culture

The Museum of the Kurpie region in Nowogród is among Poland's oldest ethnographic parks and presents the traditional architecture of the Kurpie region. Thanks to such places, this old wooden mill-wheel remains technically in good shape.

Łyse, in the Kurpie region. This small locality is known for its annual Easter "palm" contest.

folk culture

The Sieradzanie Song and Dance Ensemble presents the folk customs, songs and dances of the Sieradz, Łowicz and Lublin areas.

Maurzyce. The Open-air Museum of Łowicz Culture. The interiors of the old cottages are adorned with paper cutouts, mainly featuring plant or zoomorphic motifs. Flowers made of paper also hang from the ceiling.

folk culture

The Open-Air Museum of the Masovian Countryside in Sierpc features the folk architecture of northern Masovia. This farmhouse is one of nearly 100 artifacts on the 60-hectare site.

Złaków Kościelny. One of the folk traditions still upheld here is the Corpus Christi procession, in which people wear the traditional costume of the Łowicz region.

In its performances, the Mazowsze Song and Dance Ensemble harks back to the Polish folk tradition. Established in 1950, it propagates the music, song, dance and folk costume of some 39 ethnographic regions of Poland.

Tokarnia, near Kielce. The Museum of the Kielce Countryside has assembled a collection of rural wooden architecture, farm implements and everyday items.

Spycimierz, near Uniejów. A colourful carpet of strewn flowers adorns the Corpus Christi processional route.

folk culture

Wieliczka. An old tradition cultivated on Easter Monday that harks back to pagan times and requires a man to dress up as a woman known as *Siuda Baba*. "She" must then walk around the town with "her" entourage, dressed in folk costume and covering people's faces with soot!

Kraków. Each year's Corpus Christi procession through the city's streets (which kicks off the "Kraków Days" festival) is led off by the so-called *Lajkonik*, whose costume was designed by Stanisław Wyspiański in 1904.

The wall painting in the so-called "white chamber" of Anna Dorula's house in Szaflary is the work of an Italian artist brought to this village in the Podhale region by the parish priest to decorate the church.

Glass paintings by folk artist Ewelina Pęksowa of Zakopane, whose work graces museum collections around the world. Her art mainly features religious subject matter, but legends, customs and traditions of the Podhale region are also portrayed.

The village of Bukowina Tatrzańska in the Podhale region plays host to a national carol-singing contest. This troupe of singers comes from the Węgierska Górka area near Żywiec.

Zakopane. Highlander music is a manifestation of a living folk culture that is much beloved by visitors from the lowlands. Here, young musicians prepare for a performance at the annual International Festival of Mountain Folklore.

The Podhale region. The highly decorative embroidered bodice of a local folk costume. Red beads are an essential component, and the finest are made from real coral.

CHRISTIAN PARMA
photography

MACIEJ KRUPA
text

BOGNA PARMA
captions

ANNA CZAJKOWSKA
(CLEAR EYES TRANSLATORS)
translation of text

JAMES RICHARDS
translation of captions

ADRIAN LUKAS SMITH
English-language proofreading

WYDAWNICTWO PARMA PRESS
ELIZA DZIENIO, JOWITA KIJEWICZ
DTP

Wydawnictwo PARMA PRESS
05 270 Marki, al. Józefa Piłsudskiego 189 b
+48 22/ 781 16 48, 781 16 49
wydawnictwo@parmapress.com.pl
www.parmapress.com.pl
publisher

ISBN 978-83-7777-162-4

© Copyright by Wydawnictwo PARMA® PRESS
© Copyright for text by MACIEJ KRUPA
Marki 2019

on the cover:
Białystok. The Baroque Palace of the Branicki Family, is situated in a large landscaped park is known as the "Versailles of Podlasie".

photo on p. 2:
Kadzidłowo in the Masuria region; a stork in a local wildlife park.